Walks around Goathland

Covering 554 square miles, the North York Moors National Park is one of England's finest landscapes. Heather moors, pastoral dales and a spectacular coastline give the area unique qualities that the Park Authority strives to protect and conserve.

Published by North York Moors National Park Authority
New edition 2008
© North York Moors National Park Authority 2008
ISBN 978-1-904622-22-2

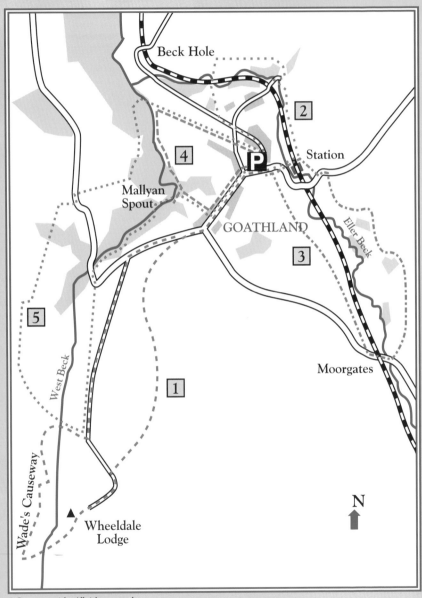

Beck Hole

2

Station

4

Mallyan
Spout

GOATHLAND

3

Eller Beck

5

West Beck

Moorgates

1

N

Wade's Causeway

Wheeldale
Lodge

About this guide

Welcome to Goathland and some of the finest walks in the North York Moors. With deep forested valleys and open rolling moorlands, superb waterfalls and picturesque farmsteads, Goathland has many hidden treasures. There is no better way to discover them than on foot.

The five walks in this guide unfold the colourful story of Goathland, from its origins as a scattering of farms to the arrival of the railway and the tourists it brought. Discover the ancient relics of Goathland's past and learn how this special landscape is cared for today. But above all, use this guide to enjoy the wonderful scenery of this beautiful area.

The walks are all circular and vary in length from 2 to 7 miles. The times suggested are generous - for people who prefer to amble rather than march. Each walk starts from the car park. Please take care when walking on roads.

IMPORTANT - Make sure you wear stout shoes and a waterproof wherever you walk in the country, as paths can be muddy and the weather can change rapidly. You should avoid walking on the moorland in bad weather, especially when misty. Paths beside streams can sometimes be flooded after heavy rain.

Walk 1   IN THE BEGINNING

The story of Goathland began three thousand years ago when the first Bronze Age settlers arrived. Follow this walk to explore Goathland's ancient past and discover its oldest remains.

THE EARLIEST FARMERS

Take a look at the moorlands around the village. Today they form a bleak, treeless landscape where only heather and a few other hardy plants grow, but thousands of years ago, the whole area was covered by a vast forest of oak, birch and hazel.

During the Bronze Age people cleared large areas in the forest for their homes and fields. They chose the high ground because it was less boggy. These areas have become the moorlands of today.

A glance at the map shows many 'howes' on the moors, marking the position of Bronze Age burial mounds. During the walk you may spot some of them on the horizon, a fitting reminder of Goathland's first settlers.

AN ANCIENT ROAD

This walk takes you to another of Goathland's ancient features, the old road known as 'Wade's Causeway'. Once it ran for many miles, but today this stretch near Goathland is all that's left to explore.

For many years archaeologists believed the road was Roman, built around AD 80 when the legions first invaded the area. It appears to link the Roman fort at Lease Rigg with that at Cawthorn Camps. Over five metres wide, you can easily imagine soldiers marching on it as they patrolled the most northerly province of the empire.

Now its origins are less certain. Some people believe it may have been built later in the Roman era and it may even have been used in mediaeval times.

HEATHER MOORLAND

Visit Goathland in late summer and you will find the moors a shimmering expanse of purple heather.

Heather has grown on the moors since Bronze Age settlers first cleared the forests. Today, the moorland is carefully managed to support populations of red grouse for shooting. Look closely and you may notice patches of heather of different heights. Grouse need a mixture of tall, mature heather for nesting and young shoots for feeding. Moorland owners systematically burn or cut areas of heather to produce these conditions.

Despite being a man-made landscape, heather moorland is a valuable environment for wildlife. Birds such as the golden plover and the rare merlin live here. The National Park Authority works with local people to conserve this special landscape for the future.

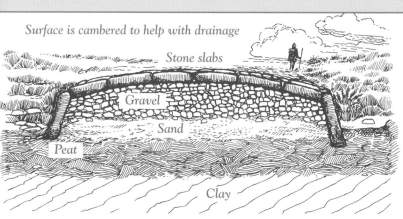

Surface is cambered to help with drainage

Stone slabs

Gravel

Sand

Peat

Clay

As you may suspect, 'Wade's Causeway' is not the original name for the road. A popular legend tells of a giant named Wade. He is said to have built the road for his wife Bell, to herd their sheep along. In reality Wade was probably confused with a Saxon thane named Wada, who was reputed to be of great height.

Walk 1

Wade's Causeway

The route follows paths over the moors to Wade's Causeway, then returns to the village along the minor road.

Time	3½ hours
Length	6 miles
Terrain	A gentle walk with one or two steeper slopes

1. Turn right along Goathland's main road towards Egton Bridge. At the first junction follow the main road round to the left.

2. Just after the church take the road on the right. After the old pinfold follow the bridleway on the left which cuts diagonally up the hill.

3. As the ground levels out continue at that level, avoiding any path which cuts uphill.

4. After crossing a couple of ditches, turn left towards the prominent cairn of stones.

5. After the cairn, turn right and follow the path through the heather.

6. Follow the path down the hillside towards Hunt House.

7. Turn left on to the track.

8. Turn right along the wall past Wheeldale Lodge. Turn right, over the stile, cross the stream and follow the path on the left diagonally up the hill.

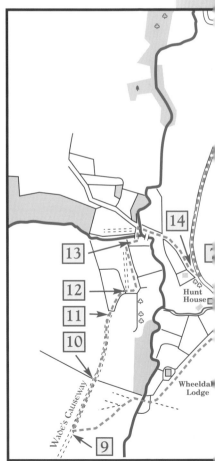

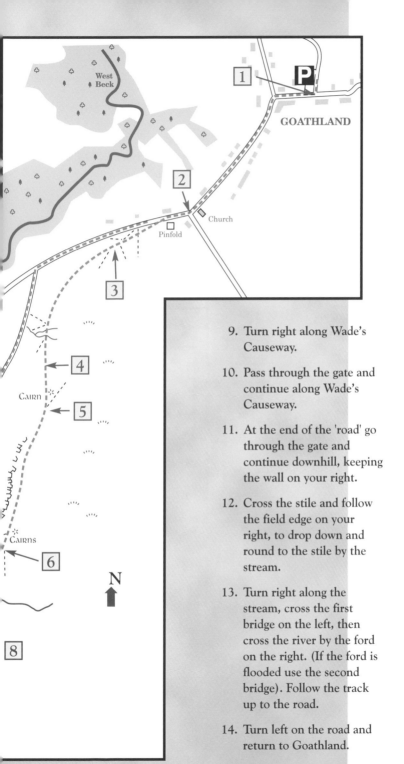

9. Turn right along Wade's Causeway.

10. Pass through the gate and continue along Wade's Causeway.

11. At the end of the 'road' go through the gate and continue downhill, keeping the wall on your right.

12. Cross the stile and follow the field edge on your right, to drop down and round to the stile by the stream.

13. Turn right along the stream, cross the first bridge on the left, then cross the river by the ford on the right. (If the ford is flooded use the second bridge). Follow the track up to the road.

14. Turn left on the road and return to Goathland.

Walk 2 FARMS AND FIELDS

For thousands of years people scratched a living from the infertile lands around Goathland. By mediaeval times a village called Godeland was established. This walk takes you through the village and into the countryside, revealing how generations of farmers have used and shaped the land.

THE BIRTH OF A FARMING VILLAGE

The first settlement to be recorded here dates from around 1100, when a priest established a hermitage by the river. From this small seed a whole agricultural community grew.

As you walk, notice how scattered the buildings are. Goathland differs from many villages because it never had a lord of the manor. Consequently, it was always isolated from the outside world and gradually grew as a scattering of farmsteads.

TAMING THE LAND

Goathland lies in a hollow amongst the moorland. Mediaeval settlers chose this site because the sheltered land was easy to farm. They used heather from the moors as thatching for their cottages.

Nowadays the landscape owes its appearance to modern farming practices, with the landowners earning income

from grouse shooting on the moorland.

Around Goathland you can see scattered fragments of woodland. In mediaeval times the woods were more extensive and they were a valuable resource for the villagers. Wood was used to make tools, furniture and clogs, and for building the timber-framed cottages.

For many years the most important building in Goathland was the mill, where the farmers would grind their corn into flour. Early in the walk you will pass a building by the river called 'The Mill'. As its name suggests it was once Goathland's mill and the flowing waters of the Eller Beck provided the power to drive a waterwheel. You can still see remains of the stone trods or pathways that led from the mill into the village.

BRACKEN

One of the most common plants you will see during this walk is bracken. Notice how it covers large areas and excludes other plants.

It grows from underground shoots and once established, it shades out other plants. Bracken is poisonous to sheep, so bracken-covered farmland is land that is wasted for the farmer.

Bracken is spreading throughout the area and during the walk you can see where it is encroaching on to the moorland. The National Park Authority works with landowners to prevent the bracken from spreading, by spraying or cutting it in summer.

Walk 2

Darnholme

Following footpaths around the village, the walk takes you alongside the river to an attractive waterfall. Make sure you pause to admire the views.

Time	1½ hours
Length	3 miles
Terrain	A few short but steep slopes

1. Turn left along Goathland's main road towards Whitby. Where the road bends to the right, take the left fork to the station.

2. Go through the gate onto the platform and, using the footbridge on the right, cross the railway to the gate opposite.

3. Go through the gate and follow the path to the left alongside the fence.

4. At the foot of the steps the path heads towards the house on the right, then swings left to the footbridge over the river. Cross and continue to the road.

5. Turn right along the road and cross the river using the stepping stones. Continue up the track.

6. Turn left over the footbridge and follow the steps up the hillside.

7. Cross the stile on the left and head towards the gate opposite.

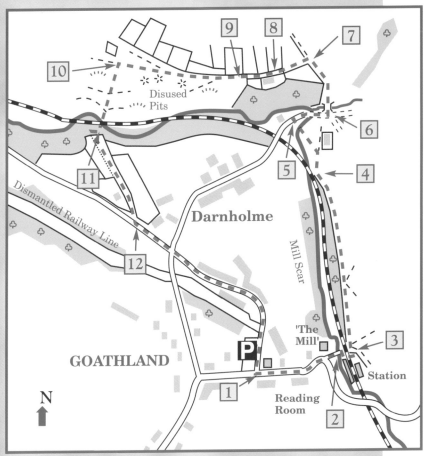

8. Continue behind the farmstead and through another gate.

9. Follow the path along the side of the wall, ignoring the path branching off to the left. Where the path touches the rim of an old pit, bear slightly left towards the largest mound 300 metres away.

10. Near the corner of the walled enclosure turn left. Continue straight down to the footbridge beneath the railway line.

11. Cross the river and follow the path up the hill, over the stile and on to the road.

12. Turn left along the road and return to the car park.

Walk 3 THE RAILWAY REVC

For centuries the farming folk of Goathland continued their quiet lives largely isolated from the outside world. The roads were poor, few people ventured outside the parish and travellers passing through were a rarity. This was to change on 26 May 1836. The Pickering to Whitby railway opened and suddenly Goathland was on a major rail route.

Walk 3 helps you explore this part of Goathland's history. Notice how level and straight the first path is. This is because you are following the route of Goathland's original railway. It was built to improve Whitby's connections inland, because the town's shipbuilding industry was collapsing. Horses pulled the first carriages but later steam engines were introduced.

RAILWAY HABITATS

Walk the route in summer and you are in for a real feast of colour. Abandoned railways such as this provide a wide strip of undisturbed land and a safe haven for all sorts of plants.

You will see a whole range of trees, including beech, horse chestnut and Scots pine. They provide sheltered 'hedgerow' conditions where a huge variety of wildflowers can thrive.

At Moorgates House you can see more evidence of the old railway. Look for the railway sign in front of the house, which reads 'Moor Crossing'. As this suggests, the railway crossed the road at this point. The house was once a pair of cottages for railway workers who manned the gates across the road.

Among the plants you can find here are stitchwort, germander speedwell and red campion. These plants thrive under the shelter and shade of trees, and can often be found in hedges and the edges of woods.

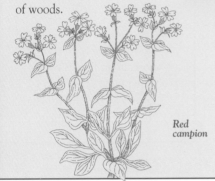

Red campion

Further along you can see railway embankments, with an arch passing underneath. The arch was built to let cattle and other livestock pass from one side of the railway to the other.

During the walk you will get some excellent views of Goathland's second railway. One of the problems with the first route was the ascent north of Goathland, which was too

steep for the horses to pull the carriages up. This was solved with a clever pulley and counterweight system but the process was slow and dangerous. Therefore, a second, less steep railway was built, with the two lines joining soon after Moorgates.

Look out for steam trains chugging along the railway. Although the line was closed in 1965, the North York Moors Historical Railway Trust took it over and brought the age of steam back to life.

At the end of the walk you will pass through Goathland's station. Today it looks much like it did in Victorian times. You can easily imagine the first visitors arriving at this village.

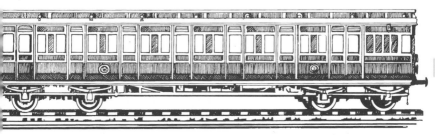

Walk 3

Moorgates

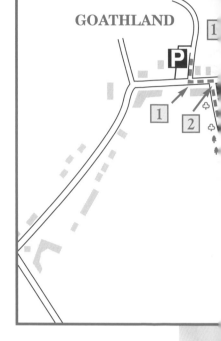

The route follows the old railway line before looping back on paths, with excellent views, along the side of the valley.

Time	2 hours
Length	4 miles
Terrain	A gentle walk on good paths

1. Turn left along Goathland's main road towards Whitby.

2. Just before the Goathland Hotel turn right and follow the bridleway for one and a half miles to Moorgates House.

3. Turn left onto the road.

4. Turn left onto the farm lane.

5. Follow the bridleway above Birchwood Farm.

6. Cross the stream and follow the side of the wood.

7. Follow the track to the road.

8. Cross the road and take the footpath to the left alongside the wall. At the corner of the wall follow the path straight ahead across the moor.

9. Follow the path alongside the wall and head downhill to the station.

10. Cross the railway by the footbridge on your left.

11. Where you meet the road continue straight on and return to the car park.

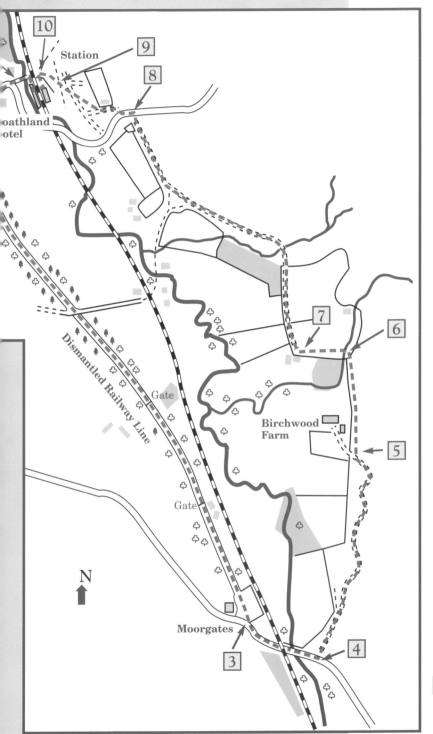

Walk 4 VISITORS & HOTELS

Until 1836, Goathland was an isolated farming village like any other. Then the railway was opened and people began to visit the village. Follow this walk to discover what makes Goathland so popular.

You only have to glance around the countryside to see how beautiful it is. Wooded ravines and pleasant farmland make Goathland an ideal place for relaxation. This walk also takes you to Goathland's most famous landmark, Mallyan Spout. Over 20 metres high, you can easily see why so many people have visited it over the years.

At the beginning of the walk you will pass through Goathland's village green, another feature to attract visitors. In 1890, Whitby Golf Club decided that the wide grassy spaces were an ideal site for a golf course. Thankfully it was abandoned in the 1950s but you can easily imagine visitors flooding here to play golf in such an impressive setting.

BRINGING THE FIRST VISITORS

The final stretch of the walk climbs uphill on a straight and even path. You are now walking on the line of the railway that first brought tourists to Goathland. You may think the slope is a gentle stroll uphill, but the carriages were pulled by horses and the 1 in 10 gradient was too steep for them.

The solution was to uncouple the horses at the foot of the hill. The coaches were then attached, via a rope around a pulley at the top of the hill, to a

MALLYAN SPOUT

Mallyan Spout helped put Goathland on the map as a tourist village. The water cascading down the waterfall rises from springs in the moorland above Goathland. It finds the easiest route downhill until it meets New Wath Scar.

This deep ravine was cut by the flowing water of West Beck, which over thousands of years has eroded a path through the sandstone. At Mallyan Spout the sides of the ravine are 20 metres high and almost vertical. Water draining from the moors has no option but to tumble over the edge, forming a towering waterfall for us to enjoy.

wagon containing water tanks. The tanks were then filled with water so the weight of the wagon hauled the carriages up the incline.

The ascent was slow and dangerous and it was eventually abandoned in favour of a more level route. You can still find evidence of the original railway. The pieces of masonry at the top of the hill are the remains of the old station. You can also tell the former railway workers' houses, such as Incline Cottage, by their characteristic building style.

17

Walk 4

Mallyan Spout

A pleasant stroll through the village and along the dismantled railway track.

Time	1½ hours
Length	3 miles
Terrain	On roads and good paths but the detour to Mallyan Spout is a rocky scramble

1. Turn right along Goathland's main road towards Egton Bridge.

2. At the junction follow the main road around to the left.

3. Turn right down the side of the Mallyan Spout Hotel, signposted 'Footpath to Mallyan Spout'.

4. At the junction, the path to the left leads upstream to Mallyan Spout. This rocky scramble should only be attempted by the sure-footed.

5. Return to the junction and follow the boardwalk through the woodland. Keep to the path as it crosses the fields and climbs high above the valley bottom.

6. Turn right up the broad incline. (For a short detour to Beck Hole, turn left along this track.)

7. Cross the road and continue along the path.

8. At the road turn right and return to the car park.

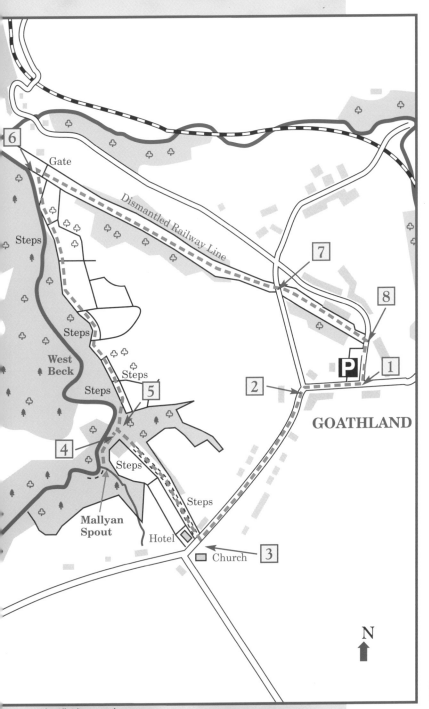

West Beck

Mallyan Spout

Hotel

☐ Church

GOATHLAND

Steps

Gate

Dismantled Railway Line

N

Walk 5 GOATHLAND TODAY

This walk helps you discover how Goathland's landscape is shaped today. The land is still worked by farmers and foresters but conservation also plays a role. Goathland lies within the North York Moors National Park, an area that is specially protected for future generations to enjoy.

firs, chosen because they grow rapidly and produce a good crop of quality timber.

The conifers cast a lot of shade and few plants live on the forest floor. In comparison it is much lighter under the broadleaved trees and there is a varied and thriving undergrowth. Today foresters plant at least 5% of their woodlands with broadleaved trees. This gives a more attractive woodland and a better home for wildlife.

A WORKING WOODLAND

Forestry has a big effect on the landscape. There are several conifer plantations around Goathland and early in this walk you will pass through one.

You can see many differences between the conifer plantation and the broadleaved woodlands around it. Notice how dense the trees are in the plantation. The trees include larch and Douglas

NEW WATH SCAR

During this walk you will pass through the beautiful woodland along New Wath Scar. Look for the fascinating plants and animals that live here.

The sides of the ravine are sheltered from the sun so they are cool and damp. These conditions are ideal for damp-loving plants such as mosses, ferns and woodrush. Look out for alder, a tree which thrives in wet ground.

The rich woodland is a home for a wide range of animals, so tread carefully. One bird you are

A FARMING LANDSCAPE

Drystone walls are a major feature of this farming landscape. Many have stood for hundreds of years and they clearly add to the beauty of the area. They are also valuable homes for wildlife. Notice how exposed the farming landscape is, with very few trees. Drystone walls are an important source of shelter and all sorts of animals live in the cracks between the stones.

The National Park Authority strives to conserve this traditional farming landscape. Support is available to help farmers maintain features such as drystone walls.

Alder

likely to see is the grey wagtail. This grey, black and yellow bird spends much of its time perched on boulders or walking at the water's edge. It feeds on insects hovering above the stream.

Areas with such a rich variety of wildlife are rare in today's crowded countryside. For this reason, the woodland along West Beck has been designated a Site of Special Scientific Interest. This means it is a very special habitat for wildlife that is carefully conserved for the future.

Walk 5

New Wath Scar

A pleasant walk through varied countryside, with excellent views of the area.

Time   4 hours

Length   7 miles

Terrain   The section of the walk along New Wath Scar is very rocky, in places becoming quite a scramble. Only those wearing walking boots should attempt it. An alternative route follows the road back to Goathland

1. Leave the car park by the exit near the toilets, turning left along the road.

2. Turn left on to the Rail Trail.

3. Cross the road and continue on the Rail Trail downhill.

4. At the signpost, follow the bridleway on the left over the footbridge. Cross the boardwalk and climb the steps into the wood.

5. Turn left and follow the stone trod through the wood.

6. At the waymark post go straight on along the footpath.

7. Where the path comes out of the wood, go straight on, keeping close to the edge of the field. Cross the stile back into the wood. At the junction turn right.

8. Cross the stile into the field. At the top of the slope turn right, keeping to the side of the wall, and follow the path to the road.

9. Turn left on to the road. After a few metres turn right and follow the road to Hollin House Farm.

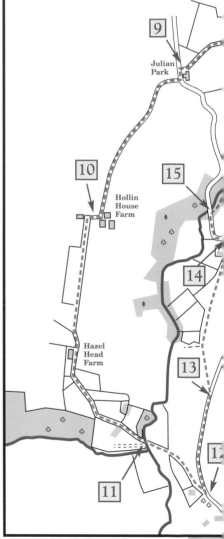

22

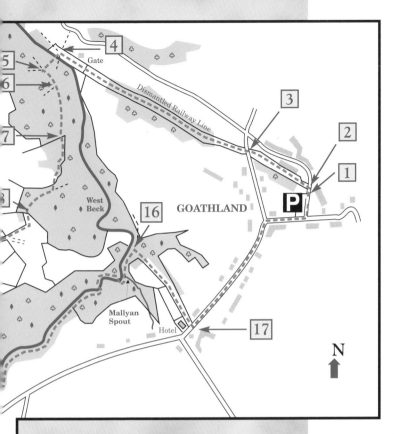

GOATHLAND

West Beck

Gate

Dismantled Railway Line

Mallyan Spout

Hotel

N

10. Turn right around the farm, and follow the track past Hazel Head Farm and down to the river.

11. Cross the river by the ford and continue up to the road. (If the river is in spate, cross by the bridge on the right, turn left to the second bridge and cross here).

12. Turn left along the road.

13. Turn left along the bridleway and follow it to the road. NOTE: An alternative is to continue on the road back into Goathland, so avoiding the rough path along New Wath Scar.

14. Turn left along the road.

15. Just before the stream, cross the stile on the right and follow the rough footpath along the bottom of the gorge.

16. Shortly after passing Mallyan Spout, turn right along the footpath, signposted to Goathland.

17. Turn left along the road into Goathland and return to the car park.

MOORS MESSAGE

Tread Gently on the moors. They may withstand all sorts of weather, but they, their plants and animals are fragile and sensitive

Fences & Walls keep some animals in and some out. Use stiles or gates and please leave gates as you found them.

Uncontrolled Fires can devastate vast areas of moorland, which may never fully recover. Don't start campfires or drop cigarettes or matches.

Litter is dangerous as well as unsightly. Take it home.

Dogs are allowed on rights of way, but please keep them at heel or on a short lead if you can't rely on their obedience. A loose dog can harm sheep and ground-nesting birds. Dogs are restricted on most Open Access moorland in the North York Moors; please follow signs at access information points

Weather conditions can change quickly. Mist on the moors is no fun. Are you fully equipped?

Footpaths are for feet. Bicycles and horses may be ridden on bridleways. Please remember that the countryside is shared and always consider others.

*Leave the countryside
as you found it,
for others to enjoy.*